# HISTORY in a HURRY

## Romans

SUNNYSIDE
PRIMARY SCHOOL

written and drawn by
JOHN FARMAN

MACMILLAN
CHILDREN'S BOOKS

First published 1998 by Macmillan Children's Books
a division of Macmillan Publishers Limited
25 Eccleston Place, London SW1W 9NF
and Basingstoke

Associated companies throughout the world

ISBN 0 330 35250 4

1 3 5 7 9 8 6 4 2

A CIP catalogue record for this book is available from
the British Library.

Printed and bound in Great Britain
by Mackays of Chatham plc, Kent

# ☁ *CONTENTS*

*Off we go!*      *4*

1 **The Historical Bit**      *6*

2 **Downtown Rome**      *11*

3 **Looking Cool**      *16*

4 **Eating Out and In**      *21*

5 **Surviving School**      *27*

6 **Fun and Games Roman Style**      *30*

7 **Slaving for the Future**      *34*

8 **Art, Culture, Science and Stuff Like That**      *39*

9 **From 'gods' to 'God' with the Romans**      *44*

10 **Emperors and What They Got Up To**      *47*

11 **The Game's Up**      *61*

*Time's Up*      *64*

# ☁ OFF WE GO!

Whoever said Rome wasn't built in a day wasn't kidding. Everyone knows it took two days (now *I'm* kidding). These are the two versions of how it all came about.

## The Unofficial Version

Once upon a time, back in 753 BC, twin brothers Romulus and Remus, the baby sons of Sylvia the Vestal Virgin (a likely story) and Mars (god of chocolate?), were chucked into the River Tiber by a very nasty piece of work called Amulius. They were washed ashore, suckled by a she-wolf and fed by a woodpecker. When grown up, Romulus went into the building business and started with Rome (most builders start with garden sheds), but brother Remus wouldn't stop taking the mickey out of his efforts and kept leaping over the very ramparts that had been specially built to keep foreign foes out. This annoyed Romulus, who slew (that's old-speak for killed) his brother and carried on regardless. Romulus made his new city a refuge for male outlaws (a bit like Miami?), but soon realized that they were rather short of women for wives (like none!), so he invited the local Sabine tribe for tea and games somewhere where the suburbs would have been had there been any. As soon as they'd finished their tea, the new Romans shooed off the poor unarmed men and dragged their women back to Rome. *The End.*

Now I don't know about you, but I started getting a little suspicious by the wolf and woodpecker bit. Most of the wolves I know* would more likely see a couple of freshly washed humanoid nippers as a light supper, and woodpeckers would like as not have spiked them to death when trying to feed 'em. As for the Sabine women bit, it's pretty much true – apart from the tea party!

**The Official Version**
Once upon a time, long before 753 BC, Italian peasants called Latins began to set up home on the seven hills that surround Rome. The Italian peninsular had been occupied from 1500 BC by people who came from the east (that's why they look so tanned), cheekily kicking out the poor residents who'd been there since monkeydom. Rome was actually built by the Etruscans, a northern people who'd pitched up in Italy in 700 BC and who, after a rather good century, were practically running the show. Etruria, as they called it, consisted of twelve self-governing cities, each of which was thus a mini-republic in its own right. Biggest and best was Rome, which, by 500 BC, had become a rather rich and highly developed (for then) trading centre. The rich, resident Romans soon became so powerful that by 500 BC, after a series of nasty battles, they kicked the other Etruscans and their rulers out. Most of the other Italian cities took their lead and did the same. That's gratitude for you.

PS. If you notice annoying scribbles by 'Ed' in this book, I'm sorry, but it's Susie, my fussy editor. The printer left them in by mistake.

*I suppose you know lots? Ed

# Chapter 1

# ⟨⟩ *THE HISTORICAL BIT*

## Two and a Half Classes

From the very outset, the Romans divided themselves into two classes; the posh *patricians* who were the aristocracy and the poor *plebeians* (or plebs), who were the common people. There was also a little class called the *clients* who basically relied on the patricians for everything, but we won't bother too much about them. At the very top were a series of elected kings with daft names like Numa Pompilius, Tullus Hostillus, or Tarquinius Superbus (sounds like an upmarket coach company). They were chosen by a group of top patricians called the Senate or Council of the Elders, who then advised – or should I say told – them what to do. Old Superbus was a right tyrant and ended up being hated by posh and poor alike. They eventually evicted him (and the whole idea of kings) for good in 509 BC.

## Vive le Républic

From this point on all the power was given to one man, who held the job for a year and was called Dick Tator*. After that, two consuls (both patricians) were elected every year to run the show. Naturally, the plebs didn't go for this too much, so in 494 BC they put all their feet down and made such a fuss that eventually it was decreed that one of these consuls had to be a plebeian.

---

*I don't want to interfere, but don't you mean dictator? *Ed*

## Rome Goes a-Roaming

Rome was still basically a smallish city, but as it became more powerful the inhabitants began gently flexing their muscles and peeking over its seven hills to the world beyond. For the next ten or so years their army did rather well and one by one all the mid-Italian towns fell under Rome's power (you have to start somewhere when you're Empire-building). But in 390 BC there was a bit of a setback. The ghastly Gauls (from roughly where France is now) broke through the ramparts (obviously Remus was right) and completely trashed the city before shoving off with all its best treasures (and girls).

You can't keep a good Roman down, however, and they soon rebuilt their city, making it bigger and better than ever. But before Rome could grow into the rich, fun-loving place that we know and love today, it had some more serious conquering to do. At that time, it was a bit of a toss-up as to whether Rome or Carthage (in North Africa) would rule the whole of the Mediterranean. Carthage controlled North Africa, western Sicily and much of southern Spain. Let's face it, it was fairly inevitable that a mighty big punch-up was a-coming. By 274 BC the Romans had finally conquered southern Italy (including the Greek bit), so they now ruled the whole country and were hungry for more.

### Useless Fact No. 403

As the Romans spread their wings, so did the Latin language (wot they spoke) – which had come from the ancient state of Latinium. Nobody speaks it now – shame, really.

But the Carthaginians were still a mighty power, and getting mightier, which really bugged the ambitious Romans, so much so that they eventually rolled up their sleeves and got down to some serious fighting. The first big prize had to be Sicily (the 'ball' that looks like it's being kicked by the Italian mainland 'boot'), but the trouble was that, unlike the Carthaginians, they had no navy to attack it with. Having no navy meant that they had no boats, and in order to have a navy, they had to find some boats.* Luckily they found an old Carthaginian wreck on a beach, which they quickly copied (the boat, not the beach) and – hey presto! – instant navy.

## Punic Wars

These Punic Wars (as they were called – don't ask me why**) went on for ages with both sides winning a bit and then losing a bit. One of Rome's greatest threats came from the mighty Carthaginian general and elephant-man, Hannibal, who, in one of the finest military achievements of all time, brought 50,000 men and 38 jumbos across the snow-covered Alps to

*We haven't got all day. Get on with it. Ed  **Why? Ed  Oh all right. Punic means 'relating to Carthage' in much the same way that Dutch means 'relating to the Netherlands'. I told you not to ask. JF

attack Italy (see Great Cold Feats). He was to keep up the pressure on Italy for twelve years.

In 203 BC Hannibal was recalled to Africa where he met and was eventually beaten by the awesome Roman general, Scipio, who, with a bigger, bolder and better-trained army finally decided who was going to rule the Med. One of the many reasons Hannibal lost was due to his elephants (now numbering 80) being untrained and rather naughty which, as you might imagine, caused complete havoc among his men. One of the snags with elephants, I suppose.

### Useless Fact No. 408
Elephants were used quite extensively in wars in those days. When Hannibal's lot first lumbered down from the mountains, they scared the wits out of the early Romans (and their horses) who'd never seen anything like them before (even at the circus).

## Greek SOS
A couple of years after the Romans' great victory over Hannibal, they got a call from Athens, Greece, asking if they could possibly help them fend off Philip of Macedon who was giving them quite a hard time. No prob, said the Romans, knowing full well that, if they did, there was a good chance that they could have Greece in their empire as well – which they eventually did in 133 BC.

## Spain Next
There was no stopping those rampant Romans. In less than a hundred years they'd roped in Spain, Gaul (France, Belgium and bits of Germany, Holland and Switzerland), Syria and the western part of Turkey, to their empire. Then their great Emperor Trajan had a go, conquering Romania (or Dacia, as

it was then) and then all the countries right across to the edge of Asia. In the other direction, they finally got to us. A swift sail across the channel, a little serious Saxon bashing, and then, before you could say spaghetti carbonara, Britain became Britannia (and Italian) in 55 BC.

THE ROMAN EMP

# Chapter 2

# DOWNTOWN ROME

As I've only got a few thousand words to create this definitive work on the hole Wholy Roman Empire*, I hope you'll forgive me for picking just one particular time in Rome's long and illustrious history (actually, it's all the same to me whether you forgive me or not). It's probably best to dive in around 1800 years ago when it was not only up and running, but at its most hip and splendiferous.

When I went to modern Rome, not that long ago, the streets were mayhem with thousands of nippy Fiats and buzzy Vespas tearing around like deranged ants. It might surprise you to know it wasn't much different in ancient times. Surrounding the magnificent civic buildings was a rat's nest of tiny, teeming, narrow streets. To be fair, they didn't allow wheeled transport during the day, but all that meant was that, when night fell, they became even more hectic (as you know, the Italians never say anything quietly if they can yell it at the top of their voices**). It must have been hell for all those poor ancients trying to get a good night's kip.

## Highly Flammable

Being a hot country, fires were all the rage and the badly built tenements would go up – and then down – at the drop of a hat (preferably flaming). Despite the laws saying that buildings could only be of a certain height, the wily Romans insisted on building precarious wooden extensions on the tops, making

*Try again. Ed
**Well done, you've managed to offend another country. Ed

the whole city a vertical tinderbox. Fire was therefore a constant nightmare for the city-bound Romans.

**Water, Water Everywhere**

Despite the fact that it was usually impossible to get water to the actual scene of a fire (no fire engines, fire hydrants or, in the early days, firemen), there was plenty to drink and wash in, as it was brought right into the centre of the city on breathtaking aqueducts that came from the surrounding hillside springs.

The Romans, like the Greeks before them, were famous for being very clean (bodywise anyway). Those with loads of money had their own bathrooms but the rest used the magnificent public baths that were to spread throughout their empire (we even had them in boring old Britannia). Actually the public baths were so fab that the rich went as well, just to show off and partake of the social life. These monumental buildings were simply staggering: vast, money-no-object marble edifices decorated in silver and gold, and filled with massive statues and paintings. Some pools took 3,000 bathers comfortably in one sitting (or should that be one 'floating'). Here the rich, who had their own personal towel-slave, and the poor, who didn't, could have a swim followed by a dip in the steaming-hot or ice-cold plunge pools.

Then maybe a sauna, a stroll in the sumptuous gardens with your mates or even a handy haircut, followed by a passable lunch. There were gymnasiums and libraries, people to massage you, anoint

you, perfume you and even, if you were a woman (or a man, come to that), pull all those little unwanted hairs out of you. All this for a *quadrans* (their smallest coin) for a whole day. Try getting anything like that down the local swimming baths. Progress? I don't think so.

### Useless Fact No. 416

The last public building to be built in Britain with anything approaching the magnificence of the bigger Roman baths was St Paul's Cathedral – and that's only a quarter of the size (and you can't get a bath there).

## Rich Houses

Most Italians who had any sense wanted to live as near to where the action was as possible. Nothing's changed here – that's why great cities like London, New York or Paris have mile upon mile of suburbs. The wealthy Romans' houses were on the very edge of the city, up Palatine Hill or on the banks of the Tiber.

First of all they would build loads of rooms around an *atrium* (courtyard), and then they'd build another lot next to it and call it – um – another courtyard (*atrium*). These houses were really big and full of valuable gear, so to keep potential robbers out they had heavily armed dogs and vicious watch-slaves (is that right?) patrolling the boundary walls.

The Roman villa owners became famous for their beautiful gardens which were based on the 'gardens of paradise' that a lot of the dads had seen out east when playing at soldiers. These were places of immense tranquillity (apart from all the din coming from the rest of the city, just over the wall) and were chock-full of ornamental fountains and statues, exotic plants and trees, birds and beasts from far and wide.

## Simply Marbleous

The Romans were marble mad and imported it from the four corners of their growing empire. They used it everywhere possible in their stylish villas, which were, in fact, more flash and comfortable than anything seen in western Europe before or since. They crammed these villas full of brilliant statues imported from the east (or nicked from Greece) and made sure that there was always enough gold and silver on display. The whole intention was to out-do their rich friends and neighbours (just like Hollywood).

Their furniture was also over the top: highly elaborate tables, chairs and couches were inlaid with ivory, tortoiseshell or gold, with legs carved like animals' paws and topped by the heads of lions and other beasts (not real ones). They were often made on the premises by their own in-house craftsmen. The walls would be covered in the finest mosaics and frescoes, while the floors (marble, of course) would be covered in the skins of deer, wolf, bear, leopard, tiger or lion (real this time, but dead – and flat).

Best of all, they had running water and – an absolute revelation – underfloor heating. This was relatively inexpensive

D'YOU EVER GET THAT SORT OF FLAT FEELING?

providing you had enough underfloor wood and enough underfloor slaves to keep the underfloor furnaces going.

## Modest Houses

The great majority of the homes that weren't owned by the rich Romans were pretty basic – usually a couple of rooms over shops, known as *insulas*. Around AD 350 Rome contained 44,173 insulas and 1,782 private dwellings. Unlike the rich, the insula tenants usually shared a lav on the ground floor, and chucked all their rubbish and slops onto the street below. Rome was sensationally smelly.

### Useless Fact No. 423

Because olive oil and tallow (animal fat) were the main fuel for lamps, and, more to the point, part of their daily diet, the poorer Romans were pretty stingy when it came to lighting their houses. (Would you rather eat or see?) So, if you consider that an average light bulb is equivalent to 100 candles, you might understand why they existed in semi-darkness (and always went to bed after the Nine O'Clock News).

### Useless Fact No. 424

When Julius Caesar came back from the civil wars, he gave a year's rent to all the poorer inhabitants of Rome and 24,000 sesterces to each of his lads (the legionaries), as a way of sharing the winnings.

As the Empire progressed, the city's population grew and grew until many of the great Roman houses and their surrounding land were split up to make more room for more people. As the gardens shrank, and the tenements took over, Rome became a city of insulas and window boxes (which it still is in many ways).

## Chapter 3

# ⧉— LOOKING COOL

Before the Republic came along, garments and ready-made cloth (wool and flax) were not that plentiful, so most of the stuff the Romans wore was woven and made up at home. Their clothes were dead simple – basically a sort of light blanket which the men and boys had made into a tunic, and which women and girls simply wrapped round their bodies. The poor would wear the itchy untreated wool, straight from the sheep's back (why don't sheep itch?*), but the rich would have theirs bleached, often using urine from the public lavatory (nice to think someone's peed on your new outfit), and then washed and softened many times.

### Useless Fact No. 427
The 'fullers', who did all the bleaching, preparation and washing, usually spat mouthfuls of cold water all over the finished garment before delivery. It was supposed to be good for them. (For the fullers or the garments?)

When Rome became a republic, much finer fabrics like cotton and silk came from the Empire. But it was horribly expensive – three pounds of gold for one pound of silk (mind, you that's a lotta silk). The trouble was that as some of these very fine materials were see-through, they were regarded as rather effeminate for chaps and quite tarty for women and so became the normal dress of the better-off prostitutes (and rather doubtful chaps).

*Why don't you ask one? Ed

Men's clothes were always white (sometimes with the odd coloured band) and they wore them short, but women (who could wear tasteful colours) had to wear them to their feet, which I think is the wrong way round.*

A heavier garment, essential for the Roman winters, was called a *palla* (for the girls) and a *toga* (for the guys). These were simply thick wool blankets and were worn wrapped round the body like – er – togas, I suppose.

## Useless Fact No. 429
The first emperor (Augustus) was a right chilly mortal and was known to wear four togas at a time. Safe from those cheeky gusts of wind.

### Fashion-Free Zone
Unlike these days, when what you wear seems to dictate very much whether you're a nerd or not, there was no Roman fashion as such, and throughout the history of the Roman Empire the style of dress remained much the same. If wealthy people wanted to show off they simply wore better quality materials and loads of beads, bangles and flash jewels. If a woman did let her hen creep up her leg**, or went out without her head covered, she was seen as a loose woman. Likewise if a chap went out in trousers he was jeered and called a right barbarian – a terrible insult (unless he really was a Barbarian).

Towards the end of the Republic, presumably to cheer themselves up as things were going so badly, brightly coloured cloaks became all the rage for men.

*You would! Ed
**Shouldn't that be *hem*? Ed

**Getting Ready to Go Out – Roman Style**

Although they didn't go much on fashion (clothes-wise), the better-off Roman women, by the end of the Republic, went through a right palaver to look good. Here's what they had to do, step by step, to get that Roman look:

1. Go to bed with a thick paste of flour and milk over face, or, even better – if they could get it – crocodile dung. Get the dung-washing slave to wash it off in the morning with scented water.

 2. Bad teeth were very non-U amongst the rich Romans (who invented toothpaste). Cleaning the teeth was a long arduous ritual, and if you were unlucky enough to lose them, falsies were essential.

3. A warm bath and rub-down by the scrubbing-slave with volcanic pummice stone was next. Then a quick massage.

 4. Cover face in white lead or chalk to look pale and interesting (and to hide the wrinkles).

5. Time for a quick tweeze of the eyebrows and any other hair (moustache, beard, etc.) by the plucking-slave.

6. Hair (on head) time. The Romans were fanatical about their hair. Both men and women were obsessed with baldness and would use anything to try to stop it: from bear fat to deer bone-marrow and, even better, a delicious concoction of minced rat heads, rat poo, hellebore (a plant also apparently good for curing madness) and a pinch of pepper. Strewth, I think I'd've gone down the wig shop.

7. Women's hair fashions were changing all the time, so hair-slaves would tease women's hair with tortoiseshell combs and curl it with curling tongs (non-electric) into the latest fashions.

8. Time for the old facepaint. Roman women used tons of it, often rather crudely, and would have more caskets and little pots on the dressing table than a pantomime dame (and the results were often not dissimilar).

9. Hide any blemishes with patches or artificial 'beauty' spots.

10. Shove on the sparklies and rush out to meet the lads.

### *Useless Fact No. 431*

Wigs were very common, and the Romans even had removable stone ones to bring their statues up to date.

A well-known poet and rib-tickler, called Martial, mocked one of his girlfriends by saying, 'You are made up of lies. When you take off your silken robes at night, you put aside your teeth and two thirds of your body.' (Don't try this comment at home, folks.)

# Chapter 4

# EATING OUT AND IN

One of the snags that always bugged the Roman empire was its severe poverty. The trouble with conquering folk is that you then become responsible for feeding them. History usually only tells us about all those fat cats living in the city of Rome itself, but the main obsession with the rest of the people was where their daily bread was coming from.

## Useless Fact No. 433

Before wheat was cultivated, the original Romans were thought to have existed on a diet of berries and ground-up acorns. (I bet there were some skinny Italian squirrels around.)

As hunger is one of the main reasons for revolt, and as many of the small farms round Rome were going bust due to the spread of cattle farming (and the ever-growing suburbs), the powers-that-be* eventually had to review the situation to prevent revolution.

## Cheap Corn

Thus in 123 BC it was decided that every month every citizen who wasn't a slave was entitled to 37 kilos of wheat from Sicily or Africa at cost price (government take note). The State, amazingly, paid for all the transportation. Mind you, it was no great gift. They covered the cost pretty painlessly by jacking up the taxation of all the provinces (called robbing the poor to pay the poorer).

*Shouldn't that be 'powers-that-*were*'? Ed

## Free Corn

But that was nothing. When Julius Caesar was trying to get himself elected, he proposed something absolutely unheard of – that the wheat should be given to every citizen free and for nothing. The last of the farmers around Rome promptly gave up the struggle to make a living by actual work and flocked into the city to get their daily bread free, like everyone else.

This new handout soon created an idleness that had never been seen before or since Caesar's reign, and realizing what a ludicrous thing he'd done, he tried to cut down the numbers eligible for the freebie. Luckily loads of chaps were being killed on a regular basis in the constant civil wars that were part and parcel of keeping a huge empire in one piece. Better still, thousands were constantly being packed off to live in the colonies. Eventually Julius got the number of dependants down to 150,000, well over half of what it had been before. However, Augustus, his successor, presumably seeking popularity (creep), promptly got them back to strength.

### Useless Fact No. 437

When Julius Caesar was having one of his famous clamp-downs against the excesses of the rich, he had inspectors touring the markets to remove the delicacies that he had banned. They also seized illegal and sumptuous dishes from restaurants and dining rooms. Imagine someone coming in and nicking your Big Mac – shocking.

Many people were so poverty stricken that they didn't have much of a clue what to do with all this free grain every month: they only lived in hovels and had no facilities for baking. They, therefore, either took their corn to one of the thousands of little bake-houses or simply sold their rations. This created the downside of the 'corn dole' as it was called. The 'grain ticket' became a ready commodity on the black market, and so, as a way of ensuring that one's subjects would be well fed, it all went a bit wonky.

## Early Brecky

The not very well-off Romans would usually start the day at sunrise with a little wheat pancake topped, if they were lucky, with salt, honey or olives. The main meal would be in the early afternoon when they got home from work and most times this would be porridge, flavoured with whatever savouries came to hand. It's interesting to note that when the Romans did get home from work in the early afternoon, that was usually it for the day. That's Italians for you.*

## The Cook House

By the first century, Rome had became a city of festering little street cafés and cook-houses with not a pizza or pasta joint amongst them (these days, that's all there is). These little hovels made our 'greasy spoons' or transport cafés look like smart restaurants and were used by both the very poorest citizens and the slightly better-off slaves (the poorer slaves hardly ate at all). Several emperors, paranoid about anywhere the poor might congregate and moan about their lot (which wasn't a lot), tried on many occasions to close these dives down, but with little success.

*Is it? Ed

## Eating at Home

As I said earlier, many think that all proper Romans lived in the lap of luxury. Sure, many did, but the average Roman ate a lot more sensibly and cheaply. Slaves did most of the cooking for the middle classes and above, but it must be said that slaves are usually lousy cooks (mine certainly is), and consequently, Roman cuisine, to be totally truthful, was nothing to write home about.

## Unless . . .

. . . you had money. (All this talk about how ordinary folk fed themselves is all very well but, you must admit, a tad boring.) Rich Romans delighted in showing off their wealth, and the best way to do it was to get your mates round for a bite to eat. The noblemen approached eating with much more panache; their banquets were legendary and often bizarre. No animal, fish or bird was safe from the Romans. If it moved you could be sure they'd eat it in one form or another.

Here are a few menu suggestions if you fancy giving a Roman-style feast.

- First some tasty starters. How's about a nice little dish of flamingos' tongues and mullets' livers. Alternatively, you could serve peahen's eggs, containing tiny little beccaficos (birds) rolled in spiced egg-yolk. Forget sausages on sticks, why not try roasted dormice for a change?
- If that's whetted your appetite, try giving them a wild boar which, when opened, contains live songthrushes (singing the blues?) or, still on a porky theme, a pig stuffed with sausages (that sounds like piggibalism) or a sow's udder in a rich tunnyfish sauce (that just sounds disgusting).

🛎 You could, of course, get your chef to do you some novelty dishes, like pork dressed and shaped to look like a goose, served with goldfish and lots of different birds, or maybe a fish made from the womb of a female pig (yuk!), or even a wood-pigeon . . . made out of bacon.

🛎 For dessert, can I suggest thrushes made out of pastry and stuffed with raisins and nuts, or quinces stuck with thorns to look like sea urchins.*

Or you could just do spag bol, a Cornetto for afters and be done with it.

### Useless Fact No. 437
The Romans thought that being sick was just part and parcel of having a good time. The guests would bloat themselves so much that they would be openly sick into bowls, to be taken away by the vomit-slave (see Bad Jobs in Ancient Rome). This, naturally, enabled them to eat and drink more – but don't try this at home.

## Free For All
The guests would lounge about on sofas with hordes of slaves to supply their every bidding (yes – every bidding), from

*Boring. I had those last night. Ed

keeping them cool with huge fans to keeping their wine goblets permanently topped up.

## Keeping Up With the Jonesiuses
Everyone would try to outdo each other with the splendour of their parties, whether it was the originality of their food, the opulence of their silver, the quality of their dancers and musicians, the smallness of their dwarfs, the tallness of their giants, the agility of their acrobats or the value of their gifts. The settings were astounding, like vast film sets. Nero's fabulous Golden House was just about the best, and even had a magnificent revolving dome which showered the guests with flowers. Whose doesn't?

## ⧉ Chapter 5

# ⧉ SURVIVING SCHOOL

What do you think about this? If Mr and Mrs Smithicus had a child that they didn't particularly want, whether it be weak, stupid or just plain surplus to requirements, they could simply kill it . . . providing – and this is the good bit – they got the OK from five (not four or six) neighbours or friends, and also providing that the poor little mite was under three years of age. Crikey, I know for a fact that I wouldn't have seen a fourth birthday if my folks had been given the option.*

Furthermore, it appears that dads could also kill their children when older, if they did anything naughty or that they didn't approve of (like not doing the washing up?). Better still, if they were short of a few denarii (silver coins) they could easily sell their kids into slavery, and many a hard-up parent did just that when the going got tough.

C'MON SON, YOU ALWAYS SAID YOU WANTED TO LIVE IN A BIG HOUSE

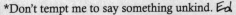

*Don't tempt me to say something unkind. Ed

## Ideals

If there are any staunch feminists out there, take a deep breath. According to the Romans, the ideal example of womanhood was she who could have lots of babies, then look after them, tend the fire, cook the food, clean the house, feed the animals, fetch the water, spin the cloth and make the clothes, all this even if there were loads of slaves around to do it anyway. This was what all little girls had to aspire to (forget being prime minister, a bus driver or a Spice Girl).

Likewise boys were expected to be little versions of their dads, be they humble farmers or top political figures. They followed them around like shadows, even to social occasions, taking in how they went about their business. I'm glad we don't do that these days – my dad sold insurance (yawn . . .).

## Schools

Oddly enough, throughout the Roman Empire, most kids could read and write. Although not compulsory, most children went to school – but don't be fooled by the word 'school'. It was often just a single room with a single, dreadfully paid teacher. (The children were given money by their parents to pay his wages.) One very famous teacher to the rich and famous, Publius Valerius Cato, died in abject poverty in a hovel, having sold his villa to pay off his debts. The Romans, you see, didn't value their teachers very highly when it came to actually rewarding them for the job (so what's new?). But even if the teachers couldn't make a living, they could at least take out their frustration on their pupils, flogging them regularly, sometimes using a leather whip as the fancy took them. (Whatever you do, don't show this book to your teacher. It might give them ideas . . .)

Home education became very popular, especially as the Romans became richer and richer and could afford private tutors. A good quality Greek slave, for instance, would fetch much more money if he could read and write, and even more if he was a good teacher.

When a boy could do the old reading and writing bit reasonably good* (girls usually gave up at this point), it was time to study Greek and literature. Having said that, the early Romans had failed to realize how lucky they were to have Greece on their doorstep. Why worry about learning all that stuff just for the sake of it, they thought. We've conquered most of the known world without GCSE Greek, so why bother now? As for philosophy, astronomy, poetry and drama – try that on a battlefield when there's some beastly barbarian about to cleave you in two.

HOMO SUM: NIHIL HUMANUM A ME ALIENUM PUTO

Translation:
I am a man; I count nothing human foreign to me.

The truth is, however, that Greek-speak gradually became rather essential for any dialogue about new scientific knowledge and, much more to the point, for trade with Egypt or with many of Rome's growing dominions.

*Unlike you, it appears. Ed

## Chapter 6

# FUN AND GAMES ROMAN STYLE

The Roman Games weren't exactly what we would think suitable for family viewing. Roman parents, however, didn't think twice about taking young Kevinus and Sharonus along for a pleasant day out. To say the Romans were cruel was like saying Hitler had a slightly less than jolly side to his nature; they invented the blinking word. And if you think the things I'm about to tell you about are a bit OTT, you ought to see the stuff I've left out (or maybe you oughtn't).

### A Family Day Out at the Colosseum

The setting would usually be some huge circular amphitheatre. The Circus Maximus, used for chariot racing, was 600 metres long and held a staggering 250,000 people. The Colosseum, which is still standing, built by Emperor Titus, seated 50,000 people. His most famous do, to celebrate its opening, went on for a hundred days. Let's take a closer look.

Practically anyone who was anyone (and almost anyone who wasn't) in Rome poured into the sweltering stadium. The posters must have been fairly eye-catching – if you're the sort that enjoys the idea of 10,000 prisoners and over 5,000 animals being slaughtered. Even the sacred Vestal Virgins, a bunch of dead important priestesses, who you'd have thought would have disapproved of this sort of behaviour, had ringside seats amongst all the noblemen and dignatories. The emperor had a private box at the very front, of course. The ordinary folk, of even more course, filled up the rows of seats right up to the back.

## Panto Time

First there was a somewhat naff cross between a pantomime and a circus, with clowns, acrobats and all that sort of thing acting out mock battles with wooden swords and pretend spears. These were all very well, but weren't exactly what the hordes had come to see – they wanted blood!

## Gladiator Time

The gladiators were 'real hard'. Ex-soldiers, trained in special schools to fight to the death or to do their master's bidding (same thing). Two teams, armed to the hilt, marched out and, at a signal from their emperor, proceeded to stab, hack and slash each other literally to pieces in front of the ecstatic crowd. In the end, all that would be left were a mass of writhing, groaning, bleeding and very much dying (or even properly dead) bodies and a few rather relieved chaps left standing up. The standing-up chaps would then saunter cockily over to the royal box for a few kind words, a bag of gold and some poxy old laurel reef (is that right?*) from the boss.

*Wreath, I think. Ed

The dead and dying would then be dragged off with hooks and ropes, and anyone still breathing finished off quickly outside. It would be some poor slave's job to remove all the armour so that it could be used again (waste not want not, I always say).

### Useless Fact No. 439
A few of these guys (obviously the better ones*) became real heroes, a bit like rock stars. At an amphitheatre in Pompeii archaeologists found a piece of graffiti which, when translated, read, 'Celadus the Thracian makes all the girls sigh.' (It doesn't even rhyme.)

### Zoo Time
Time for a change. Out of the massive doors at the side of the ring poured hundreds of weird and wonderful animals, many of which the Romans had never clapped eyes on before – ostriches, giraffes, gerbils, etc, who thundered round the ring thinking they were free. Dream on. What was the point of animals – alive? Roman archers, true to form, burst into the stadium and proceeded to slaughter them in a mad frenzy.

### Jumbo Time
Bit of a clearing-up necessary, followed by the entrance of two huge bull elephants with steel-tipped tusks, who lumbered in simply to be goaded into fighting each other until one lay dead and bleeding in the sawdust. As a treat, the winning jumbo was presented with a tethered slave for afters, who, slightly perturbed to say the least, was trampled to a pulp by the frenzied beast. But treats don't last for ever, especially in Ancient Rome. The poor old jumbo was then speared and shot full of arrows until himself dead.

*Obviously! Ed

## Supper Time

As the 'games' pressed on, more and more people and animals would be forced to fight to the death until, with a fanfare of trumpets, the climax to the day's proceedings was announced. Picture the scene: two or three hundred ragged Christian prisoners from the war in Jerusalem shuffle into the open, blinking in the brilliant Roman sunlight, looking around slightly apprehensively. Suddenly, a horde of extremely peckish lions and tigers (they'd been given no breakfast) slide menacingly into the arena from the other side, fleetingly inspect the menu (oh no, not Christians again) and then, without further ado, pounce on their unarmed lunches. After some time, all that is left is a load of rather well-fed beasts and the bloody heaps of the rather well-chewed prisoners (or ex-prisoners, I suppose).

Finally, as the sun sets in the west, each little Roman family would stroll home, tired but happy, while the arena is cleared up and re-sanded, spick and span for more fun tomorrow.

And we think boxing and fox hunting are barbaric!

# Chapter 7

# ≈ SLAVING FOR THE FUTURE

One of the best things about conquering the indigenous peoples of just about everywhere you go is that, if you play your cards right, and providing they're not all dead, you end up with loads of nice fresh slaves. In the early days, most of the Romans' slaves were Italian (hardly surprising) but by the first century BC they were pouring in from Spain, Asia, Greece (the brightest ones), and even a few from dear old Britain (the thickest ones). When they got to Rome they would be herded together in markets like cattle, totally naked (also like cattle) with signs round their necks advertising their strengths and weaknesses (not like cattle). By Trajan's reign in AD 98 there were 1,200,000 Romans and 400,000 slaves (that's about a third of a slave each, by my reckoning*). The Romans, in fact, had more slaves than any other people in history.

*Your maths really is coming on. Ed.

## Useless Fact No. 441
After one battle, Aemilius Paullus managed to sell 150,000 of the inhabitants of Epirus (northern Greece) which was, unfortunately, nearly all of 'em.

## Exchange and Mart
There were other ways of becoming a slave. Girls in ancient Rome were regarded as rather a burden (no comment, eh lads?) and if for any reason they were still unmarried by – say – seventeen, they could be sold as slaves by their fathers (I must tell my daughter that – she's way past her sell-by date). This state of affairs was seldom reversible – once a slave always a slave, I'm afraid.

## How Much is that Slave in the Window?
Like most things slave prices went up and down according to supply and demand. If the Roman legions had had a few good away matches, there'd be loads on the market and the price would go down. If, on the other hand, they weren't doing too well, the price would soar. Say you're a Roman and you're thinking of going in for a new slave, here's a rough price list:

- You can pick up a low-class, not very good-looking girl slave for less than 150 denarii (the price of a few good quality fish).
- If you want something a little more presentable, you *can* pay anything up to 2,000 denarii.
- A skilled worker will also set you back 2,000 denarii.
- A handsome boy slave might cost 2,500 denarii, but beware. If your wife is caught doing things with your new slave which are, er – how shall I put it – outside his normal duties, you can burn said slave alive. A bit of a waste of

money, you might think! Not necessarily. It's perfectly OK to then sell your wayward wife into slavery and presumably buy a nice new one (slave that is). Nothing gained, nothing lost.

If you want your girl slave to be able to sing, dance or even play a musical instrument you might have to go as high as 4,000 denarii.

At the top end of the market, you can bid against other rich people for the most desirable slaves (particularly babe slaves). Sometimes the bidding went as high as 50,000 denarii, the price of a fine house, and in one case Quintus Catalus paid 175,000 denarii for a highly educated slave.

## State-Owned Slaves

It stands to reason that most of the slaves captured in war belonged to Rome itself. This meant that there was always a ready supply of totally free workers to build all the bridges, aqueducts, roads and public buildings, etc. They also kept the streets tidy, cleaned the loos, and also did more general civil service work – even the really dirty jobs like tax collection. One of the great advantages of having slaves in responsible jobs was that if they stole anything or didn't work hard enough, you could torture or kill them at will, which beats just about any incentive-to-work scheme that I've ever heard of. Having said all that, the slaves who worked in the city had it easy compared to those that worked in the country on chain gangs. These poor souls were chained up day and night, and kept underground.

## A Few Good Things You Could Use Slaves For

- Putting out fires. Slaves formed most of the fire brigades (when they were invented), which was rather sensible. Why waste precious water if you can throw a few slaves at a fire.
- Feeding lions. Slaves were a good, plentiful, nutritious meal for the Romans' many hungry pets.
- Street decoration. After the great slave rebellion in 73 BC, led by Kirk Douglas (and played by Spartacus in the movie . . . I think), thousands of severely dead slaves were hung on poles all along the Appian way, leading south out of Rome.
- Protection. A rich man would surround himself with a gaggle of slaves if he ventured out after dark. This worked on the theory that if anyone attacked, the slaves would get it first.
- Leisure. Most rich houses employed slaves to carry out every single function, leaving the master and mistress with 100% of their time to do what they liked best (which was probably telling the slaves what to do).
- Public status. The best way of impressing your mates and society in general was to own a large number of slaves. These days we do it with servants (well, I do anyway!)*.

*And just who are you kidding? Ed

## Freedom

Sometimes an individual slave became indispensable to his owner and therefore took more looking after – and that usually involved money. In Rome, during Julius Caesar's reign, wheat and water were provided free to 'free' men like me and you (unless you're reading this in prison*) but you had to pay for anything your slave consumed. Clever slave-owners would therefore weigh up the profitability of each slave and would free them if it was worth it. Also, much-favoured slaves were sometimes given pocket money to do with as they wanted, and seeing as their living expenses were nil (one of the few perks of slavery), they could save it up. Many slaves eventually bought their freedom off their masters, especially when they were old and knackered. The other side of the coin was that many slaves lived a much better lifestyle than if they were to leave the protection of their masters. It's all very well being free, but not if you can't earn enough to live, for gods' sake (small 'g' and plural for their gods, notice).

### Useless Fact No. 444

Towards the end of the Empire, eight out of ten of the inhabitants of Rome had slave blood in them. (Those ex-slaves must have got about a bit.)

*It's bad enough being in prison, never mind having to read this stuff. Ed

# Chapter 8

# ART, CULTURE, SCIENCE
# ≈ AND STUFF LIKE THAT

Although by nature the early Romans found that the Greeks' obsession with materialism and generally having a good time went a bit against the grain, as their empire rolled on, all their art and culture became too much to miss out on. It wasn't that the Romans really understood how all these beautiful artefacts had come into existence – or even cared, come to that – it was just that the actual collection of all things Greek became a fantastic status symbol. The Greek craftsmen, of course, could hardly believe their luck, and had a ball selling everything they could knock out to the nouveau riche and nouveau pretentious Romans.

They all became so obsessed with statues that they developed a habit for depicting all their leaders and heroes (and even their friends) in statue form, and, although a little cagey at first about total nudity (not even a fig leaf involved), soon quite liked the idea.

### Useless Fact No. 447
Looking at Ancient Roman statues, you could be fooled into thinking that all posh Romans had exactly the same bodies – right down to the naughty bits. No way. The sculptors were making so many of these naked statues that they ended up producing standard bodies (well, two *different* standard bodies, of course), which they stocked up and then simply shoved appropriate heads on, sculpted to order, when required.

Roman houses (see chapter 2) were also built along the lines of classical Greek architecture to begin with – loads of columns and porticoes in the Doric or Ionic styles. Later the much more fussy Corinthian style broke through (which had been too elaborate for the Greeks to manage).

## Books and Literature

Despite all the wonderful stuff the Ancient Greeks had written (odes and odysseys and the like), the early Romans weren't that fussed about books.* Instead they had papyrus rolls which were copied over and over and over by armies of . . . copy-slaves.

WHY DOESN'T SOMEONE INVENT PRINTING?

## Hard Lines

Oneoftheproblemswiththeseancienttextsisthattheyhadnopunctuationorspac esbetweenthewordsandthewritingwasextremelytinyThismeantthatthatmany ofthescribesandscholarshadtoquittheirworkquiteearlyintheirlivesastheireyesi ghtsoondeterioratedandglasseswerenotinventedtilllateinthethirteenthcentury

*Maybe because they hadn't been invented yet. Printing and proper books didn't come along till much later. Ed   Whoops. JF

## All the Rage

Later on, however, collecting the writings of the Greek greats became 'the thing' for rich Romans to do – they'd probably got bored with collecting all those statues and paintings. Just as there are libraries full of unread books in modern posh houses, if you wanted to be seen as a cultured member of Roman society, it was essential to have a library of your very own. So bookshops (or scrollshops) sprang up throughout Rome and its provinces. Eventually the middle classes became interested in reading too, and by the end of the empire many vast public libraries existed (25 in Rome alone) – often attached to public baths (see Soggy Reads in Ancient Times). It's safe to say that the common folk were rarely seen to enter their lofty portals (fair enough, as no one had actually taught them how to read). If you'd given a scroll to a poor person, he'd probably have looked a little puzzled and then taken it off to the lav (if he had one) – and used it in a far more practical way than reading . . .

## Rhetoric?

One of the subjects that featured big in Ancient Rome, and one that we never seem to hear of these days, was called 'rhetoric'. Young better-off Romans would be required to learn public speaking and debating in such a way as to be persuasive and forceful. They would also be required to write in the same way.

## Music

Unlike the Greeks, the Romans, especially the Republicans, never really saw the point of music, unless it was to accompany some much more exciting pastime (like fighting or orgying). Anyway, playing or singing was far too 'common' for the average Roman.

They thought much the same about dancing, but if the odd good-looking slave-babe got up and started shaking her bits about, there didn't seem to be that many objections. Speaking from an intellectual's point of view, Cicero, the great Roman public speaker (and spoilsport), remarked, 'Hardly anyone who is sober dances, unless by chance he is insane; neither when he is alone, nor in any temperate and respectable gathering.' I wonder if he'd just seen *Riverdance* (armless prancing).

## What's the Time?

Telling the time had always been a problem in Ancient Rome. They did have primitive sun dials but how on earth did they know whether or not they were late for a date when the blinking sun had just gone in? The nearest they got to proper time-telling was with the Greek water-clocks that came in around 159 BC, but these were difficult to read.

## *Useless Fact No. 449*

When the first sundial was brought to Rome from Greece, they couldn't make it work properly. What they didn't realize was that one set up to work in Greece wouldn't be set up to work in Rome. It took 'em a hundred years of studying to work that one out.

## History?

It was a bit the same with the calendar. How can you begin to learn history, for instance, if you don't know about dates? The Romans, when trying to find out how long it takes for the moon to circle the earth, or the earth to circle the sun, didn't do that badly. Badly enough, however, to have to shove in a couple of weeks, or even the odd month, every now and again, to make the books balance. It was Julius Caesar (that clever geezer) who introduced the twelve-month calendar beginning on January 1st 45 BC, and that was used right up to 1752 when another clever geezer found it to be a few days out and in need of a slight tweak.

## Postscript

It is fair to say that the great age of learning which rose to such heights with the Greeks dwindled rapidly with the Romans, plummeting like a lead Zeppelin when their Great Empire collapsed.

# Chapter 9

# 🐾 *FROM 'gods' TO 'God' WITH THE ROMANS*

Although the Romans are known for establishing one of the first 'civilized' cultures, they still had a nasty habit of worshipping an awful lot of the funny old gods that they'd inherited from the Greeks – though they gave them nice new Greek names (Aries, the god of war, became Mars; Aphrodite, the god of love, became Venus, etc.). Not only that, but there seemed to be countless in-house gods to be appeased. For a start, Roman kids often had to witness the ridiculous spectacle of their parents prostrate in front of the fireplace in the morning. No, they hadn't gone barking mad – they were paying homage to the god that lived in the hearth, called Vesta, goddess of fire (and, presumably, of matches). All food and provisions were protected by spirits called *penates*, who apparently lurked in the larder (rather than the Lada). There were far too many of these protective spirits to mention, as it was generally thought that the more gods a Roman brought into the house the

PSST! WANT A COUPLE OF NEW GODS TO WORSHIP?

better – a bit like collecting conkers.* When stuck for new ones, they even promoted some of their emperors to this lofty position – as a special treat.

### Useless Fact No. 451

Emperor Vaspasian (one of the later ones) took being deified (godded) well in his stride. As he lay dying, he remarked casually to a mate, 'My goodness, I think I'm turning into a god.' (I think I know the feeling.)

## Old Mother Cybele

One of the most popular gods in the highly male-dominated Roman society was the great mother goddess Cybele, who allegedly came from the land of Troy. Her more fervent followers enjoyed a rather peculiar custom at her annual festival. They would cut their own rude bits off under the nearest pine tree, after which most of them would bleed to death. Ah well, it's a day out.

## Bacchus

The Romans certainly weren't going to let this Greek god go. Bacchus was the god of wine and, way back from Greek times (when he had been known as Dionysus), wild drunken parties were held in his honour. These *Bacchanalias* made our modern raves look like vicars' tea parties. In Livy's *History of Rome*, he describes them thus:

*'When the wine had inflamed their minds . . . depravity of every kind used to take place . . . The violence was concealed, however, because the shrieks of those tortured could not be heard over the loud wails and the crash of drums and cymbals.'* (Oasis have been going longer than I thought.)

*It's absolutely nothing like collecting conkers. Ed

The Romans never saw the need to bring all these various gods together into the big sort of religions (Catholicism, Judaism, Islam, etc.) that we go in for these days – until, that is, they began to pay more attention to those Christians that they'd had such a brilliant time persecuting.

## The Big G

The early Christians were forced to meet in back rooms of private houses, but when Constantine proclaimed his support for Christianity in AD 313 all this changed dramatically. Suddenly hard cash flooded in from everywhere and, before long, magnificent churches sprang up with unrivalled finery and decoration. God (the Christian God, that is) had won, and from then on his supporters' club grew and grew until his was the principal religion throughout the empire.

# Chapter 10

# EMPERORS AND WHAT THEY GOT UP TO

Rome's leaders were an amazing bunch. Their individual power was so huge and unquestionable that they could do anything they wanted – *when* they wanted. Here are a few of the most famous emperors, and some of the dreadful things they got up to (they did a lot more dreadful things but my editor wouldn't let most of it in*).

## Augustus, 63 BC–AD 14
*Julius Caesar's nephew, formerly known as Octavius*

The very first Emperor was Augustus. Though not nearly as off the wall as many of those that followed, he had a strange beginning. He was supposed to be the result of his rather careless mother's liaison with a snake while asleep. Here are a few interesting facts . . .

🐚 Augustus had a neat way of dealing with opposition. He organized the assassination of 300 senators and 2000 knights whose only crime was that they weren't desperately keen on the triumvirate (three-way partnership) that he had formed with Mark Antony and the little-known Lapidus to rule the empire.

🐚 Mark Antony, Augustus' partner in world domination (they soon got rid of old Lapidus), was a bit of a lad by all accounts, and he fell hook, line and sinker for a flash babe called Cleopatra (queen of Egypt). To cut a long story (and

*Too right. Ed

two people) short, Augustus got hacked off when Antony started giving his new girl bits of Roman territory, and so declared war on him. He trashed poor Antony's navy at the great sea battle of Actium in 31 BC causing Tony and Cleo to do a runner. It all ended rather badly when they became separated. Antony, believing Cleopatra to be dead, topped himself, while Cleo (who'd only been taken prisoner) preferred a fatal lovebite from her pet snake to being paraded round Rome in the back of Augustus' flashy victory cart. Seems like snakes got all the action in those days.

🐌 Augustus was credited as being the man who turned Rome from sun-dried bricks into marble. Not only that, but he gave 16,000 lbs of his own gold and 500,000 of his own gold pieces, besides jewels and pearls, to restore the

temples, which had been vandalized (by the Vandals). Mind you, you've gotta have it to give it, I always say.

🐌 He introduced the bizarre practice of sewing a person accused of murdering one of their family into a sack with a dog, a cock, a snake and a monkey. Rather unfair to the others I think.

🐌 Later in life, he was an infamous dirty old man and even used his missus to scour Rome for pretty young girls to entertain him. That's wifely love (or fear) for you. Not only was the geriatric pervert attracted to young girls, he did his best to attract boys as well.

 He was known to soften the hairs on his legs with red hot walnut shells. (Whatever turns you on, Augustus).

## Tiberius, 42 BC–AD 37
*Caligula's uncle*

Though quite a good and relatively sane emperor when young, as Tiberius got older he became weirder . . .

 He would request bevies of young girls and boys to be sent to the Isle of Capri to cavort in front of him in groups of three. Sometimes he'd make them dress up as nymphs and Pans and prance around the mouths of the caves and grottoes (sounds rather jolly). The walls of his villa would be smothered in rude pictures – just to create the right atmosphere.

 One woman called Mallonia, who refused to succumb to Tiberius (if you know what I mean), had to suffer a trumped-up criminal charge. During her trial, Tiberius continually yelled 'Aren't you sorry?' The poor woman obviously thought that anything was better than going home with him and promptly stabbed herself to death while calling him a 'filthy-mouthed, hairy, stinking old beast'. (Say what you mean, Mallonia.)

 Tiberius was stupendously mean and obsessed with money – mostly other people's! He would persuade his mates to leave him everything in their wills and then make their lives so unbearable that they'd kill themselves (cruel but surprisingly effective).

 Another trick was to confiscate the wealth of rich foreigners, claiming that they were hoarding it in order to start a revolution against him.

 He wasn't very nice to his grandchildren either. Having recommended young Nero and Drusus to the Senate, he became miffed when prayers for their safety were added to the long string of his own. He quickly blamed them for everything and saw to it that they were made public enemies. Poor young Nero committed suicide in exile, for fear of a particularly irksome execution and Drusus was starved to the point of eating the flocking out of his own mattress (tasted flocking awful). Their bodies were chopped into so many pieces that poor old Caligula (coming shortly) had trouble collecting them all up for burial.

🛎 Tiberius developed a real taste for executing people on a whim. Anything from beating your slave, changing your clothes near to a statue of his step-father Augustus, taking a coin with Augustus's head on it into the lav, or making any criticism of Augustus whatsoever, got the thumbs down.

Golly, I hope we don't ever give our Royals that sort of power (or any power, come to that) . . . I'd be dead within minutes.

🛎 Tiberius's great pleasure was to sit on the cliffs of Capri, drinking red wine, munching cheese and onion crisps*, while watching his near terminally-tortured victims being pushed over the edge. Just in case they weren't quite dead on arrival at the bottom, he had a few of his guys finish them off with oars and boat-hooks.

---

*I've warned you about getting carried away before, Mr Farman. Ed

🕭 His other great buzz was to invite groups of men to have a drink with him. When they'd drunk copiously and were beginning to look rather urgently for the Gents, he ordered their willies to be bound up so tight that they couldn't pee, presumably bursting their bladders. He was such a laugh.

## Caligula, AD 12–41

*Son of Germanicus, nephew of Tiberius*

Caligula means 'bootikins' or small boots, but the reason's too boring to go into. Don't be fooled by the dinky little nickname, however: he was probably the very naughtiest and nastiest of all the Roman Emperors . . .

🕭 Caligula is believed to have throttled his uncle Tiberius in order to become Emperor, and then to have crucified the only eye-witness (see Sensible Moves in Ancient Rome).

🕭 The masses became deliriously happy when they found out he was to replace his wicked uncle Tiberius but little did they know what they were letting themselves in for. When he accompanied his dead uncle to his funeral they affectionately yelled such names as 'star', 'chicken', 'baby' and 'pet', which I personally would've have found a bit insulting. He preferred names like 'Father of the Army', 'The Greatest and Best of Men' and the much more dubious 'Son of the Camp'*.

🕭 When he was made Emperor, the Romans sacrificed 150,000 captives just to make the party go with a swing.

🕭 One of his most amazing (and most daft) feats was to build a bridge, for no apparent reason, across the gulf of Baiae – a distance of three miles. But it wasn't any old bridge; Caligula had every available merchant ship (the merchants must have been delighted) anchored in two close-together lines and then boarded across the gap. Earth was

*Probably sounds better in Latin. Ed

then piled on the planks until a long, thin dirt road was created. For two days he paraded across in his best charioteer's outfit and in his flashest chariot with all his guards and best mates following behind.

When the bridge was finished he invited a large group of spectators to inspect his handiwork. For a bit of fun, he tipped them all into the water and when they tried to climb back on the boats, he had them pushed away with boat-hooks so that he and his chums could watch them all drown.

Having been intimate with two of his sisters, he managed to marry the youngest, Drusilla (having nicked her off her husband). He left her everything in his will, including his empire (how kind), but she died before him. He then, rather oddly, made it a hanging offence to laugh, wash or eat with any of one's family during the period of public mourning.

He wasn't the best wedding guest. At the marriage of his mate Gaius Piso and Livia Orestilla he cheekily sneaked off with the bride. When he was fed up with her, he banished her for ever. Worse still, he once sent for the Consular Governor's wife because someone had mentioned that her grandmother had once been a great beauty (dodgy odds, eh lads?). He soon got bored, however, and rather meanly ordered her to stay celibate (look it up) for ever (even though she was married).

Just for a lark, he used to ask quite innocently after the whereabouts of chaps he'd secretly murdered and disposed of only a couple of days earlier.

Caligula had some very odd ideas on entertainment. He would order feeble old citizens or slaves to fight equally feeble old lions and tigers – just for a laugh. Sometimes, just to slow the pace even more, he'd make respectable, but severely disabled, householders fight to the death. Imagine if all that went on now! All those protection groups like Help the Aged and the RSPCA would blow a gasket.

🎩 If anyone was unwise enough to mutter a word against his entertainments or question his 'genius', he would:

a) send them down the mines

b) jam them in tiny cages on their hands and knees

c) throw them to his animals

d) let them die in agony from a thousand small cuts

e) saw them in half (if a bit pushed for time).

Which one would you choose?

🎩 One of his knights, sent by Caligula to become lion food, screamed out his innocence. The good news was that he was brought back to see the boss. The bad news was that Caligula cut his tongue out and returned him to the now rather impatient beasts.

🎩 Caligula became so crazed with his power that he went into weird flights of fancy, like levelling mountains to flat land, building towering mountains where there had been none, and driving endless tunnels into the hardest granite, all as quickly as possible ... even if not possible. If something wasn't carried out in the time he'd said, he'd execute all concerned (which was obviously half the fun). In one year alone he squandered 27 million gold pieces on such follies – everything Uncle Tiberius had left him.

🗿 Caligula fell out with one of his senators and asked all his colleagues to stab the poor chap with their pens when he entered the Senate – then lynch him. Which they did. He further asked, if it wouldn't be *too* much trouble, to have the defunct senator's limbs and guts dragged through the streets and then dropped in a neat pile at his (Caligula's) feet. Keep Rome Tidy, I say!

🗿 Because he was balefully bald of head and horribly hairy of body, he made it a capital offence for anyone to look down on him or to even mention goats in his presence. Having said that, he often went out in extraordinary and laughable outfits – often women's wear* – presumably safe in the knowledge that no one would dare giggle.

🗿 Caligula was eventually murdered by his own soldiers, who stabbed him through the private parts. His subjects had been so terrified of him that for ages after his death, nobody dared say what they really thought of him in case it was all an elaborate trick to find out . . . what they really thought of him! He had ruled for just under four years. Four years of terror and extravagance the equal of which the world had never seen.

## Claudius (10 BC–AD 54)
*Nero's father by adoption and Caligula's uncle*
Claudius' mum once rather uncharitably described her son as 'a monster: a man whom Mother Nature had begun to work upon, but then flung aside.' He'd always been rather a pathetic

*What's laughable about women's wear? Ed

kid, sickly and definitely behind the door when the brains were handed out. He soon gave up any hope of a political career but was strangely popular amongst those in power, especially Caligula who made him his right-hand man. Here are a few facts . . .

🐌 He got the big job at fifty, almost by accident. Before murdering Caligula, his assassins ordered the courtiers out of the room. Claudius left too – fearing something was afoot. He hid behind a curtain, and when all was quiet, a soldier who happened to be strolling past noticed Claudius' feet, drew the curtain back . . . but then, to Claudius' surprise, fell on his knees and pronounced him emperor.

🐌 Everyone used to take the mickey out of Claudius and whenever he turned up to dine the throng would pretend that there were no spare couches. When he fell asleep, which he always did after eating and drinking, they'd all pelt him with bits of bread and olive stones – just for kicks.

🐌 Unlike his predecessors, he was extremely courteous to his people. He was also very fair, which made him quite popular. But if he found someone guilty of a particularly nasty crime, it was straight down to the wild beast department.

🐌 Although in some respects a gentle man, don't go thinking that he didn't go in for all that torture stuff like the others. His lust for watching his fellow man being roughed up knew no bounds. And no one was allowed to get away with faking injury. Any gladiator who fell on purpose (or even accidentally for that matter) had his throat cut instantly.

🐌 Claudius managed to conquer Britain without ever having to get his sword out – there was practically no opposition. He returned triumphant to his Roman subjects. I bet the Nazis had wished it was as easy as that.*

*You just won't let it lie, will you? Ed

He was a terrible glutton and would more
times than not eat and drink so
much that he would fall on his
back with his mouth open –
completely unconscious. His
servants would then drop a feather
into his mouth causing him to
retch and throw up the lot.

Claudius liked watching his
animals eating his prisoners, so
much so, that sometimes he would
sit alone from dawn to dusk in the huge stadia watching the
fun. If they ever ran out of victims, he'd use the stagehands
or theatre assistants, anyone he could find. Seems a shame
to waste good animals, I expect he thought.

He was somewhat absent-minded. Once, having just
executed his wife for alleged adultery, he asked his courtiers
why her ladyship was late for dinner that night. Hey-ho.

### Nero (AD 37–68)

*Claudius' nephew and adopted son*

Nero was the last of the really dreadful emperors, and in some
ways managed to outdo the rest of them. His father, Gnaeus
Domitius, was rather unpleasant himself. Once, while
thrashing his chariot through a village, he deliberately aimed at
– and killed – a little boy for fun. When one of his knights
brought it to his attention, with just a hint of criticism, Gnaeus
personally gouged his eyes out. As for Nero himself . . .

He was very poor when young, on account of his uncle
Caligula nicking his inheritance. He was educated by a
dancer and the local barber and ended up admittedly not

very bright but a bit of a groovy mover . . . with rather nice hair.

- Nero's biggest buzz was entertainment. He loved huge, extravagant parties, spectacular stage plays, massive gladiatorial contests, competitions in music, athletics and bingo.* He would give away fabulous gifts: anything from exotic caged birds, food hampers, clothes and jewellery to slaves and his own tame lions and tigers. He even gave away tenement blocks and farms – if in a particularly good mood.

- Strangely enough Nero forbade killing during these spectaculars but got a great kick from making his senators and noblemen fight each other in the ring.

- Nero was the first to start punishing a small, new-fangled sect called Christians. Didn't seem to hold them back much, did it?

- Nero was never wild about expanding his huge empire (he was having too much fun with the one he had) and thought that Britain, for instance, was a waste of time and effort (comments on a postcard, please).

- He was always setting up musical competitions purely for himself to win. He loved Greece particularly because the creepy Greeks would always give him first prize for lyre playing (what liars) or singing. Sometimes he was even known to bribe the other competitors to perform badly. Nobody was allowed to leave a concert if he was playing and his performances were known to go on for so long that some poor women actually delivered babies and some men, so excruciatingly bored, collapsed and pretended to be dead.

- That was the public side of Nero. The other side was not nearly as jolly. At night he would pull on a huge cloak and slip into the streets in search of real danger. His favourite

*Don't be silly, Mr Farman. Ed

thing was to attack innocent drunks on their way home from a night on the town, stab them and drop them into one of Rome's voluminous sewers. He'd also rob shops and houses and, can you believe it, open little in-palace stores, selling all he'd plundered. What a little monkey he was.

🐀 Things got much worse as he got older. His wild feasts lasted all day and he'd invite all the loose women and dancing girls from far and wide to perform. Even when he went on little boat trips down the Tiber, he organized for there to be temporary houses of ill-repute with naked girls enticing him from the banks (Westminster, Midland, Lloyds?).

🐀 But that was nothing. As well as trying it on with his mum, Nero went through a strange marriage ceremony with a young man – parading him through the streets of Rome, wedding dress, veil and all, in his magnificent chariot.

🐀 He was completely reckless where money was concerned and really admired old Uncle Caligula, for squandering his Uncle Tiberius' massive fortune without giving a single penny away to the needy (charity certainly *didn't* begin at Rome). Nero never wore the same clothes twice (nor do I)*, gambled 4000 gold pieces on every spot of a dice, never travelled with less than 1000 carriages, had his mules shod with silver, built a 40 metre statue of himself and had a back

*No – you wear them thousands of times. Ed

garden with a pool the size of a lake and every kind of animal (wild or otherwise) strolling about. His 'Golden House' defied description, except to say that it was probably the most sumptuous that Rome or the world had ever seen.

Spend all that money and what happens? Bankruptcy, of course. Nero decided to get it back by grabbing the estates of all those that he thought hadn't shown him enough respect, or who hadn't bequeathed him enough loot. He even recalled most of the presents that he'd given to major cities as a reward for giving him prizes in rigged competitions. He spotted one woman wearing a colour that he had earlier banned (cheeky); he had her dragged off and relieved of all her clothes and, naturally, all her property as well.

Later, he became an enthusiastic poisoner. His victims included his father, Emperor Claudius, who'd adopted him (that's gratitude for you), his half-brother Britannicus and his auntie Domitia.

When he didn't fancy his mother any more, Nero tried many ways of getting rid of her. One was a collapsible ceiling over her bed (but someone gave her a tip-off). Then he gave her a collapsible cabin cruiser, designed to sink on the slightest collision (but this time she swam ashore). Eventually he sent someone called Agermus (with dagger) to do her in properly (no nonsense). Please don't try any of this at home.

Lastly, he executed his new wife Octavia, and married Poppaea (*not* the sailorman) whom he then kicked to death because she complained when he came home late from the races. I don't know what the world was coming to; if a chap couldn't have a night out . . .

Nero, like most of the emperors before him, got a real taste for death and soon no one was safe. If he didn't like someone, he politely ordered them to commit suicide, and if they were a little slow about it, he sent his private 'doctors' in to help.

By the end everyone loathed Nero and there were several assassination attempts. But when he heard that the Senate itself were out to execute him in the traditional way – stripped naked and beaten to death with sticks – he stabbed himself in the throat, begging his guards to bury him in one piece.

There were a few rather boring emperors after these, but I've been far too indulgent with this lot anyway, according to my editor, and we're in a hurry so we'll push on. But if you want to know lots and lots more about these awful emperors, and if you don't care about holding on to the contents of your stomach, there is a book called *The Twelve Caesars* by Gauis Suetonius Tranquillus (but it wasn't me that told you).

# Chapter 11

# = THE GAME'S UP

Although the decline of the Roman Empire came as a bit of a surprise to all concerned, when it actually *fell* hardly anyone really noticed. Strangely enough, before the decline, the empire had had a rather nice century, with five jolly good but slightly ordinary emperors – Nerva, Trajan, Adrian Wall,* Antoninus and the dead clever Marcus Aurelius.

It all started going wobbly in AD 192 with the murder of Marcus Aurelius' horrid boy Commodus (inventor of the portable lav?). There was a period of great confusion leaderwise, which was not so good because the beastly barbarians were running amok, constantly nibbling at the border formed by the rivers Rhine and Danube. In AD 286 the whole Empire was split across the middle – east and west – because it had become too much of a handful to control from one place. Emperor Diocletian (sounds like a surgical instrument) took the east and Maximilian the west.

But the barbarians weren't their only problem – there was this sparkly new religion called Christianity, the followers of which, despite heavy persecution (if you call being made into pet food, persecution) were beginning to get a stranglehold wherever they went. On the basis that if you can't beat 'em, join 'em, the Romans eventually made Christianity the official religion (but not until after they'd done in its leader, Jesus). And Emperor Constantine got made a Christian on his

*Shouldn't that be 'Hadrian', and wasn't the 'wall' something he built? Ed   Anyone can make a mistake. JF

deathbed – just in time to go to heaven (funny how many people do that). The downside was that they had to look elsewhere for animal fodder.

## So What Was Wrong With Barbarians?
Despite a few nasty habits (see especially Chapters 10), the Romans were quite a civilized bunch, and didn't like the Barbarians one little bit. (Dictionary definition: rough, wild and uncultured peoples. Romans' definition: anyone who didn't speak proper, i.e. Latin.) They disapproved of them so much, in fact, that it practically cost them the Empire just keeping 'em out.

But what was so bad about them? Well, for starters, they smelt terrible to the rather refined Roman nose. For seconds, unlike the Romans, they only needed a couple of bevvies and they were blind drunk. On top of that, they played appallingly grumpy Gothic music, and worse than all that – as if their hair wasn't dirty enough, they smothered it with extra grease.

However, the straw that broke the camel's back, the habit

that upset the Romans most of all – and I hope you're ready for this – was the fact that all the men wore . . . trousers. Urghh!

## All Down to Cash

So how did the Empire eventually fall? Well, it was the western bit of the Empire that started to go a bit shaky. The financial drag of shelling out for all those armies constantly playing away started to become a bit of a strain, and to make things worse there was a terrible trade recession throughout the Mediterranean. On top of this, there was a serious drop in the birthrate (I wonder if that had anything to do with the Christians and their Ten Commandments).

Eventually things became so tight, moneywise, in Rome that bribery and corruption multiplied enormously, and the rot affected every layer of Roman society. But more importantly, the Romans started losing their battles and worse still, their bottle. By the fourth century AD those blinking Goths (Germans to you) were crawling all over Europe, while the Angles, Saxons and Jutes had more than just an eye on occupied Britain. And then there were the Huns, and then there were the Lombards, and then there were the Burgund . . . well, you get the picture. Fairly black by all accounts.

Eventually, in 410, the Goths reached Rome, ransacked it and went home. In 451 it was the Vandals' turn. Rome didn't give up without a darn good scrap, however, but in 476 they were totally trashed by the army of the German Odoacer who shooed out the last Roman Emperor in the west, made himself King of Italy and promptly ended the Roman Empire – game, set and match. Oh well, they'd had quite a good run, I suppose.

# ☁️ TIME'S UP

Any proper historian would throw the book (preferably his) at me for even attempting to tackle such a mighty subject as the Ancient Romans in 64 pages. If he did, I would calmly and politely point out that my mighty volume cost little more than a couple of bags of chips (salt and vinegar included), and that my readers, whose time is no doubt extremely valuable, won't and don't have to drag through page after page of boring detail to get the point.*

I am actually joking. If you really want to find out a whole lot more about the Roman way of life I suggest you trundle down to your local library. You could do far worse than read FR Cowell's long and comprehensive *Everyday Life in Ancient Rome* – I did.

But, dear reader, if you want to move swiftly on (and you've another couple of quid to spare), might I suggest you try one of the other books in my series. With a bit of luck, I should have written 'em by now.

---

*I must have missed it. *Ed*